The
MARKETING
Side Of
RESTAURANTS

How To Get Your Business Media Coverage
And Be Smarter Than Your Competitors

Copyright © 2022 Clifford Bramble, Jr.

VIII

CLIFFORD BRAMBLE

Professional Praise

"The Marketing Side of Restaurants is the handbook to navigating past the superficial trappings of the restaurant business and getting to the real story about why your guests will care."

- Caren West, President, Caren West PR.
www.carenwestpr.com

"This book is a must-have for anyone who wants to increase business at their restaurant. Cliff has not left out a single rule, suggestion, or good marketing idea that I can think of! I am definitely going to buy copies to hand out."

Melissa Libby, President, Melissa Libby & Associates
www.thinkmla.com

"For those neophytes that are looking to build a restaurant business, this primer is an excellent clear and concise step-by-step guide written by a revered industry expert."

- Valerie Failla, Founder, Via Failla Marketing
www.viafailla.com

"I have been in PR and branding for some of the best. One thing often lacking is restaurant management studying basics. So many are in survival mode these days. All the more reason to make a point to buy and READ this book. So much is covered, and it's so needed!"

Toren Anderson Public Relations
www.torenanderson.com

"Many restaurants know they need PR + marketing but don't truly understand what it is, what it does + how to do it. This book is an incredible blueprint no matter what stage of the restaurant game you are in. From pre-opening to post-opening, Cliff makes it that easy!"

– Tara Murphy, Founder, 360 Media, Inc.
www.360media.net

All rights reserved. No part of this book may be reproduced in any form or by any electronic or mechanical means, including information storage or retrieval systems, without express permission in writing from the publisher, except by a reviewer, who may quote brief passages in a review. Scanning, uploading, and electronic distribution of this book or the facilitation of such without the publisher's permission are strictly prohibited.

Please purchase only authorized electronic editions and do not participate in or encourage electronic piracy of copyrighted materials. Any educational institutions wishing for bulk orders, presentations, photocopy parts, or all the work for classroom use, or anthology, should send inquiries to the QR code below. To protect the privacy of individuals, names, occurrences, and locations have been omitted. Any resemblance to actual persons, living or dead, business establishments, events, or locales is entirely coincidental. Questions can be sent to sales@hungryhospitality.com

Contact

Website

Copyright © 2022
All Rights Reserved
ISBN: 978-0-9856892-6-1
Printed in the United States of America
FIRST EDITION - 2022
Published by Hungry Hospitality LLC
hungryhospitality.com

A special thank you to my wife and kids for listening to my thoughts, reading and correcting pages, and understanding how an entrepreneur thinks.

INDEX

This book is packed with tiny bits of information and is such a fast and informational read we decided not to add an index. Instead, start at the beginning and finish the less-than one hundred pages in no time. We hope you learn many new ideas to help you market, publicize, and get more people in your restaurant.

****

Over the years, while training others, I was tired of repeating myself, so after publishing my two books, I took them and created online mini-restaurant business courses.

The courses make it less expensive to learn the restaurant business and help develop our future leaders faster. Available for anyone interested in learning including, businesses, students, entrepreneurs, and restaurants.

An online Restaurant Industry Academy at www.coursini.com

Scan the code to go to the site. (www.coursini.com)

A Restaurant Industry Academy Offering Mini Business Courses

****

A QUICK THOUGHT

In the past two years, restaurants have had a tough time. It has been in the news hundreds of times. According to the National Restaurant Association, over one hundred thousand restaurants have closed, including mine. This is part of the reason I decided to write this book: ***This book helps restaurant owners, operators, chefs, students, and future restaurateurs market their businesses.*** It's one way to help others who have experienced the same issues I have experienced.

I know this: *Restaurant owners and operators are resilient.* They will bounce back, and the restaurants will be busier than ever. So, if there is one thing you can do for the person you know in the restaurant business, it would be to **hand them this book.** Regardless of their experience, it will assist them.

Over the past thirty or so years, I have been involved with several high-profile restaurants as owner and co-owner. Before opening, I planned for years. The planning was for every part of the business. But, most importantly, one area I spent a lot of time in was marketing the restaurant. **My goal was simple.** Gain the most attention and recognition from the media with the hopes of filling the restaurant or coffeehouse nightly. After all, media *credibility fills seats!*

I started planning at least five years before a restaurant even opened. For example, in the early nineties, I would go to the Newport Beach library or Barnes & Noble and take photos of the magazines I thought I could get coverage. I also began collecting every magazine masthead along with every editor and publisher's name. I took those names and created a spreadsheet of their names and the publications. Then, I added their emails and phone numbers to the spreadsheet. The emails were what interested me. I knew I now had a direct line to them, and whether they opened the email or not, they were going to read the subject line. The subject line was the key to getting noticed. Provide a great **subject line**, and hopefully, the email will be read.

How did I increase the number of emails on hand? I always had the website up and online for six months before the business opened. Then, I added a pop-up window on the website's home page. The window asked people for their emails. I ended up with over ten thousand emails!

Before email, I would create press releases and fax them to news stations and fax numbers I pulled out of a phone book. (Yes, fax numbers were in phone books!) Of course, none of those people receiving the faxed press release knew I was sending them from a hot two-car garage, a steaming hot attic, or one of Providence's dimly lit, dirt-floor basements. But, it worked, and several of my businesses were featured in many magazines. Those press releases and the articles that followed kept the company in the news & busy. It all started with an old-school fax machine!

Lastly, before a restaurant opened, I had already collected thousands of emails that assisted in direct email marketing. The emails included media contacts, industry people, chefs, managers, event managers, and hotel executives. The press coverage my first coffeehouse received prompted me to create a press logbook along with the photos and the articles within the magazines. There was so much publicity and articles written about the restaurant, I had to stop and think about how to pitch the next idea. (I had a list of ideas to present.) In Providence, the rumor was I had hired a large publicity company. (That was me sitting in a dirt-floor basement along with a fax on a wobbly table.) That method of collecting data is the inspiration for this book. It's like the saying in Gladiator, "Win the crowd, and you win your freedom." Except I say, "Win the press, and you win guests." Enjoy the book.

ABOUT THE AUTHOR

I have always said, "I am one of the nerdiest restaurateurs around. I don't have any tattoos, don't smoke, and hardly ever drink." Oddly enough, I serve all those that do. I landed in the restaurant business and have always had a passion for finance, marketing, and the industry. My marketing background started in Orange County, California, where I got my first taste of business marketing. I was amazed how a press release faxed to the local news station resulted in a six-o'clock news story. Now, after thirty-five years of promoting a business and companies I have co-owned, it was time to share this knowledge with others.

Previously, I was recognized by the Georgia Restaurant Association as a Restaurateur of the Year. In the past, I co-founded one of the best steakhouses in the United States and have been featured on *Capitalist Sage, The Power to Adapt*, and the *Peachtree Corners podcasts*. In addition, I was instrumental in getting the restaurants or coffee-houses recognition locally, regionally, and nationally in magazines like Atlanta Magazine, Rhode Island Monthly, Veranda, Food & Wine, Travel & Leisure, Details Magazine, Playboy, Gourmet, Orange County Magazine, Esquire, National Geographic, Wall Street Journal, Southern Living, USA TODAY, and more. The top celebrities, from actors to sports players to past presidents, dined in the restaurants. Their names are in the daily headlines.

With over four decades of restaurant and hotel experience in casual, upscale, and full-service restaurants, I acquired my business foundation with Marriott Hotels. From 2004-to 2020, I co-founded and operated successful independent multi-million-dollar, profitable restaurants throughout Atlanta.

My prior background includes founding a coffeehouse in Providence, RI., and co-founding Atlanta restaurants Rathbun's, Kevin Rathbun Steak, Krog Bar, and KR SteakBar. I assisted in building those businesses into multi-million-dollar profitable and award-winning companies which received local and national recognition.

Until June 2020, I also owned Noble Fin Restaurant in Gwinnett County, Georgia. Covid-19 forced the closing. Noble Fin was recognized as the best restaurant in Georgia's second-largest county.

My reach of the American dream was not without hardship. When I was in my teens, in the dead of winter in Rhode Island, I kept warm in front of a newspaper log fireplace with my Mother as she explained to me, "While we do not have much right now, we will bounce back." We did.

Then, in my early twenties, I suffered several devastating blood clots to my legs and could not walk for six months. Finally, the doctor told me they wanted to amputate my leg, and I would never walk normally again. I fought the decision and won. It took months of rehabilitation, but with my determination, drive, and self-motivation, I began walking without a wheelchair or crutches.

Currently, I own Hungry Hospitality (HH), a restaurant and marketing consulting firm. Under the HH umbrella, I have created a Restaurant Industry Academy called Coursini. In addition, we market this book and the Amazon best-selling book ***The Business Side of Restaurants*** to small businesses, restaurants, and hotels.

Originally from Rhode Island, I believe anyone can achieve their desires in life. They have to set the goal, work towards it, and ***never give up***. No matter how many times one stumbles, one must continue to push for their purpose and set their sights on accomplishment. The opportunities are available; one has to find them and capitalize on them.

Oh, one more thing: I have included some Real-Life stories throughout the book. There are so many to tell, and these stories are always interesting.

PUBLIC RELATIONS

****

1

This first chapter is an overview of how a publicist can help you. Get your pens ready and write your notes on the pages you are interested in reading twice.

SHOULD THE RESTAURANT USE A PUBLICIST?

The answer is yes! I don't even have to call a friend for help on that one.

Unless you have a ton of time, are fully aware of pitching *editors,* or have an extensive *list of editors, writers*, and *magazines* in which you would like to be featured, it would be wise to hire a publicist. Publicists help your business **gain credibility** by writers writing about the business. Credibility helps a restaurant gain their **perception from their guests**. Once that happens, people want to frequent the place of business. Plus, people believe what they read in newspapers or online. Think about it. One article or review can change what people think of a restaurant. (Think about a poor health inspection.)

How much could business increase? For example, if you have a story written about you in Travel & Leisure Magazine, and your customers are **business travelers**, your business could increase dramatically. You may also gain excellent credibility. It's different from marketing. On the other hand, marketing is the *intangible work* that gets you into the magazines.

Here is another example. If a local food critic writes a restaurant review, the review may increase sales and brand recognition. However, if no one reads the article, the sales will not change. In the nineties, and before the Internet, the newspapers were the only outlets to be read. So once a restaurant review came out, the restaurant would typically be packed for the next six months. Unfortunately, that does not happen as much, especially since the readership of newspapers has decreased tremendously. Even my fourteen-year-old son says, "Old people read newspapers."

Hiring a publicist is the best idea if you are opening or re-opening a restaurant. Again, the reasons are simple: They know how to get the word out to their contacts, hoping their contacts will write about the new opening.

Additionally, they have relationships with journalists! They also have credibility with editors and magazines to which they have previously pitched a story. They may also have the editorial calendars of future articles for the local magazine. Anybody can attain this, but it takes *money, time,* and *effort* to get noticed.

Something to think about: If you join a chamber of commerce and have one thousand members, how long will it take to build a rapport with them? It will be years. In a restaurant, you do not have much time, so hiring a publicist and getting recognition in front of thousands will help you gain more guests & credibility at a faster rate.

A few ideas:

For the business owner, if you hire a publicist, I would recommend the following:

- Meet with your publicist twice a month. During the meeting, hand them a list of items you are working on and thinking about for the next three months.
- Ask them to pull editorial calendars or search future articles on the topics, and pitch your story to the editor. How will they know what you are working on if you do not feed them information?
- Provide the publicist with information that will help them sell you. That is why you have hired them.

Keep this in mind: Who really gives a shit that there is a new menu item going on the menu? Sorry, I am blunt here, but it's been pitched a million times before. That's your job to post it on IG or FB or have your social media person do it for you. Your job is to be creative and assist the publicist with coming up with something *different*. Get down to the real **story** of an item and create something totally off the wall. Not food. **A story!** Let's take a look at what a publicist can do for you.

MEDIA KIT

A publicist can produce a digital media kit for the business. It will include press releases, previous stories from magazines, (credibility) story pitches, (ideas) photos, pdf formats of menus, a *story* of the chef/owner, and a fact sheet of information. In addition, it provides information on the respective company. This media kit can be placed on your website too.

Magazines also have media kits. However, they are really for their advertisers and rarely on their main webpage, so you have to search their site for them. Look at the very bottom of the website page under "advertising." It includes their demographics, circulation, website visitors, and much more for magazines.

A business should have something similar listed on their website too. The more information available online, the easier it will be for someone to write about it.

FACT SHEETS

The fact sheet should have the who, what, where, and when information. Add as much information as possible to it and use it on the website too.

FACT SHEET EXAMPLE:

RESTAURANT FACT SHEET

Address:

Phone:

Fax:

Email:

Owner:

Website:

Dress:

Reservations: Recommended for dinner - Lunch is walk in availability (no reservations needed)

Architect & Design:

Menu: Seafood, Steaks & More

Chef de Cuisine:

Social Media:

Logos and images:
dropbox.com/images ?TBA
(Allows them to get them immediately)

Hours:

Monday through Thursday:
Lunch 11:00-2:30
Dinner 5:00-10

Friday & Saturday
Dinner 5:00-10:30

PRESS RELEASES

The press release will be the who, why, what, when, and interesting tidbits of information within the page. Once the release has been written, it can be sent to the editors and writers. The goal is to pique their interest enough to write a story about your business. Below is an example. Keep in mind that a newly opened restaurant or new business is easy to get media coverage. A five or ten-year-old restaurant, not so much. Either way, the example is the opportunity for you to promote yourself or your business with the hopes of being included in an article.

*PRESS RELEASE EXAMPLE

FOR IMMEDIATE RELEASE

BEST-SELLING BUSINESS BOOK SETS OUT TO HELP THE RESTAURANT INDUSTRY

THE BUSINESS SIDE OF RESTAURANTS
BY CLIFFORD K. BRAMBLE, JR.
A restaurant business book

Atlanta, Georgia – When Restaurateur Cliff Bramble began writing his new best-selling book, *The Business Side of Restaurants*, he did not know the industry would be suffering the way it is today. Now, he says, "This book is exactly what restaurants need right now. It shows restaurateurs and management areas to retain their staff and increase their productivity and has eighteen steps to help businesses increase their profits. If a restaurant is not paying attention to the items in the book, they will continue to lose staff & money." It appears others agree as it has made number two on Amazon's **Best-Seller** list and became Amazon's number one **Hot New Release**.

Cliff says, "My recent tour of Atlanta tells me first-hand what is about to happen with restaurants. Based upon the apartments going up everywhere, along with companies like Google, Microsoft, Mail Chimp, Apple, and Airbnb moving to Atlanta, these companies will need more dining options. Add to this the new hotels in Atlanta like the Epicurean Hotel, Wylie Hotel, Reverb Hard Rock, and Bellyard Hotel, and you get a tremendous influx of transient business-people needing dining options." So, while the atmosphere for restaurants may not be the best right now, restaurants are not going away. The demand will still be there, which is precisely why *The Business Side of Restaurants* can help individuals in the hospitality industry.

FYI - MARKETING VS. PUBLIC RELATIONS

In a nutshell, marketing should be done daily, and many times, it's done by the owners of small businesses. Public relations is where information is sent (fed) to the media with the hopes of getting a featured story.

PROVIDING INFORMATION FOR EVERYONE

One way for writers to get easy access to your press information is to add it to your website. (Okay, some publicists won't agree with this, and I completely understand.) This includes a fact sheet, bio's of the owners, photos of the product or space, and information about the business that can make it easy for a writer to gather information. The reason is over the years, I have personally been told the number one obstacle for writers is acquiring information and images from the people they are writing about. Seems crazy, right? You would think it would be the opposite.

Make it easy for writers to write about your business and give them access to what they need. An option is making the web page private, so the writer has to punch in their email to get on the page, but I am not a fan of limited access. A barrier may scare away potential writers. The reason for this is to know who is going to your press page. Have you ever heard of this next topic?

****

EDITORIAL CALENDARS – *Old School* *See the example on page 18.

Almost every major magazine has an editorial calendar listed on its website. What is the editorial calendar? It's a monthly overview of the topics the magazine will be featuring. They show the upcoming articles they will be writing about and the months of the publication. If you are doing your marketing, your job would be to locate the calendar and send the companies a press release on what you are doing. Hopefully, it will coincide with the article being mentioned.

Would you like to locate your favorite magazine's editorial calendar? Go to Google, search for your *"magazine name,"* and then look for their **editorial calendar**. It will show in the search results. Pretty amazing and easy, right? Now multiply that by one hundred, and you will see how much time it takes to research the stories. Hire a publicist!

Over the years, I have always pulled magazine editorial calendars. I would go to the magazine's website and search for its advertising section. Once located, the editorial calendar is typically there too. I would download it and save it on my desktop.

The wonderful thing about having this in your hands is knowing you can reach out to the editor or writer and pitch (present a story idea) a story that coincides with the topic being featured. Typically, the pitch would need to be sent to the editor at least three months in advance (especially if it's a magazine). After that, the pitch can be sent to the person writing the article, the editor, or, if you have a contacts number, it's always better to call them and pitch the idea to them over the phone. Then, once you gauge their interest, you can send them the press release and backup information.

How do you know who is writing the article? Good question. I would look at the magazine covers masthead and extract the editor or writer's name. Once I got it, I would go to the LinkedIn profile and search for them. I would also tag them on Twitter and send them docs. One thing is for sure. If you stop trying, you will not get press. Suppose your goal is to get an article written about the restaurant, chef, or a topic the magazine will be covering. Don't ever stop trying,

CLIFFORD BRAMBLE

and keep in mind the editor needs something to write about, so it may as well be your place, right?

***Example of an editorial calendar

****

BEST OF LISTS

If you are ever wondering how to get on the best of lists produced by some of the top magazines in the United States and the world, here is a little helpful hint. (Other than Muck Rack & Cision)

Start by going to Google and searching for the **"Best Steakhouses in the United States."** See page 20 for results:

For example, the results lists the magazines and websites that report or select the steakhouses. Like the following: Robb Report, Gayot, Thrillist, 247 WallSt, Food Network, Travel & Leisure, Forbes, Chicago Tribune, Fox News, etc. These magazines select the best steakhouses *every year*. So, if you have a steakhouse, your job is to contact the person *writing the article* and get included on one of these lists. If you choose the respective page, the writer's name will be listed, and sometimes if you click on or hover over their name, you may get lucky and get their email.

Now, do the exact search for "Best seafood restaurant in America" or "Best restaurant in America." You can even mix it up and search for the "Best steakhouse in the United States." Of course, the search results will be different, but it gives you the information you need to market the restaurant. This is all part of working with your publicist and helping them feed the press with your information.

The other part of this search results is looking at the month these articles were published. So, for example, if the magazine was published in November, for consideration to be in the article, provide the information to the writer by July.

Last thing. Keep in mind Google's search coding frequently changes, so the results may be consistently different. The search results are based on image names, a responsive site (one that changes size based on the device), website keywords, location of the search, and website updates. So, the more stagnant a website is, the more it seems to be lower in the results.

Best steakhouse search result example.

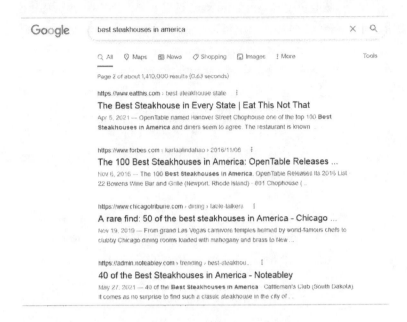

HOW GOOD WORD-OF-MOUTH GOES BAD

There are many avenues for a restaurant to receive excellent recognition. We will be discussing good word-of-mouth marketing in an upcoming chapter. This is another form. For example, one restaurant I opened became so busy so fast; guests could not get a reservation. It continued for six months. I would hear people say, "You can never get in that place." While it's great for the restaurant, there needs to be a way for the locals and regulars to secure a reservation, otherwise, they will go elsewhere. That is precisely what started to occur.

After six months of people telling others they could never get a reservation, they began going to other restaurants. So loyal guests stopped trying to make a reservation, which of course, is another issue. So, IMO, the best thing to do is something I implemented at another restaurant. I would block out a set number of reservations for the local and VIP crowd and ensure they always had a table. One note here: No restaurant I know of ever failed because they took one more table on a busy night. If a regular diner is ever calling you for a reservation and they dine frequently, my advice is to take them or suffer the consequences of poor word of mouth.

FOOD WRITERS/EDITORS

Nowadays, food writers are everywhere. There are food blogs, food writers, video blogs, and the list can go on and on with the Internet. If the restaurant is new, the best advice would be to get the press information into the food writer's hands. (Publicists do this for you) Then, possibly invite them in for a tasting or a regular dinner. *Keep in mind:* A food writer or critic will write about ***their experience***. So, watch what you wish for and be on your game because a review can go either way.

EDITORS – (Publicists know them)

If you are planning on completing the press info yourself, the one area where you will get *free* information on editors and writers is going to be on Twitter. If you search for the editor you are looking for and locate their name, you can now look at the people following them. Most of the time, it's other editors. Use it to your advantage and create a list of editors or writers that may assist or write about your business. Once you have the list of editors, organize them, and begin sending them information with the hopes of getting noticed. If you realize how much time this takes, go back to hiring a publicist!

CHARITABLE EVENTS – (Everyone calls the publicists for this)

There always seems to be a charitable event or food tasting event on the horizon. The publicists will often ask the restaurant if they would like to participate in the event. The reason is simple: The restaurant will most likely be "mentioned" in the press materials by participating in the event. This does not equate to thousands of people running into a restaurant. What it does is create *brand awareness* for your restaurant.

Keep this in mind. You can say no at any time. Many times, it seems the only types of businesses doing these events are restaurants. Have you ever seen a Proctologist giving out free exams? How about a dentist handing out free cleanings? I haven't. You will hear the event planners say, "Oh, it's free, and all you have to do is hand out enough food or beverage for 500 people." They are not telling you the **food and labor cost you money**. If it's a paid event, the event planners should be paying you the food and labor costs. Even if it's not a paid event, you should ask the planner for payment for the cost of your food and labor. If not, *every event will cost you money*.

While most business owners do not log the cost of each event, if they did, they would see it costs a considerable amount. The only one making the immediate money is the event organizer. (Maybe you should create your own annual event?)

TRADE OUTS (Pass on this)

I have two items to mention here. First, when the salesperson arrives and tells you they can do a trade-out of food and beverage for an advertisement in their magazine, say thanks but no thanks. Here's why. The first one is to know every piece of food purchased costs the restaurant money. So, salespeople sitting and eating for free will probably aggravate you.

Secondly, every piece of food you cook or buy costs the restaurant money in labor. *Food and labor are not free.* So, my two cents here is to skip the trade-outs. They typically cost you twice as much as you think.

LOCATION MARKETING

****

2

This section will discuss how a location silently helps in marketing. Check it out:

Without question, the best marketing a restaurant can receive may be from the location. It's too easy, right. Secure the site and hang a temporary sign in the front saying "opening soon." From there, the sign does the rest. Visually, the sign is all you need. Once people see the sign, they automatically know a restaurant will be opening. People's psychology takes over and creates their thoughts of interior design and menus. If it was only that easy.

If it's a great location and thirty-thousand or more cars drive by daily, it's a great marketing tool. But, on the other hand, if the restaurant is located in the back of a building and cannot be seen, the location would not be a consideration for marketing, never mind a restaurant. So, the location is one of a restaurant's most critical marketing areas.

There are great locations, and there are poor locations. Many times, the site may depend on the concept in mind. The restaurant owner should know who the restaurant will appeal to and where the location should be placed. As for lighting, there should be a well-lit parking area designated for the restaurant, and there should be either housing or business parks/buildings/hotels to support the concept. Do your best to locate the best location. Keep in mind: You want to be in an area *where people are now*, not where they will be in *ten years*.

LOCATION FACTORS

Since indirect marketing is part of the location, the placement of your business will be critical. If you are looking for a restaurant space, the following marketing factors should be considered before securing the lease.

RESTAURANT LOT ENTRANCE

Typically, there should be at least two ways to enter/exit a parking lot. If not, and there is only one easement, guests may complain about entering and exiting the restaurant.

STREET CLOSURES – (Business killers)

A recommendation is to call the city building and zoning department and ask them for their upcoming street closures or maintenance schedule. If construction happens on the street, it may cause negative word of mouth, especially with street closures.

BUILDING RENOVATION – (Negative vibes)

Sometimes it's not what is said but what isn't said. So, before signing a lease, ask the landlord about renovation plans and ask them to place them in writing.

A great example is if you move into the restaurant and the landlord decides to sell, and the new owners want to renovate, any construction in your building/area/lot will affect your business. Anytime construction is being done on a building, especially a restaurant, the perception may be the restaurant is closed, creating negative word-of-mouth.

PATIO SPACE

Depending on the concept, a patio may be needed. A patio creates excellent word-of-mouth. Customers will talk about the patio even before they drive to the restaurant.

PRIOR TENANT USE - (Second generation)

If the space were a prior restaurant, you would inherit the goodwill of the previous guests. (Consider it the driving pattern.) In addition, this helps with the conversations about the location and the directions to the restaurant for future guests.

On the other hand, if several restaurants have already closed in the exact location, you may stop and ask yourself, is it the space, the location, the concept, or the landlord? What you do not want is a guest thinking, "Oh, that location must be bad because so many restaurants have failed there."

FREE-STANDING BUILDING

A free-standing building is an excellent word-of-mouth opportunity, and it's the best-case scenario for a restaurant. In addition, free-standing allows you endless parking opportunities, especially for private functions.

FIRST FLOOR VS. SECOND FLOOR

This topic should be a non-starter. First-floor restaurants will be more successful than a restaurant where guests have to get in an elevator or climb stairs. If the restaurant space is not on the first floor, do an immediate about-face and walk away. Second-floor restaurants create negative conversations.

PARKING SPACES

This is the most crucial issue for a restaurant. The goal is to have at least two percent of the restaurant's total square feet set aside for parking. This does not mean a parking deck. This means close-by parking where a guest can walk into the restaurant easily. Parking decks are never friendly to restaurants. If you do not have enough parking, you may need to rent parking across the street, which costs money.

Think about it. It's always best to have parking around your building and within proximity to the front door. Guests do not like to walk from a garage, a large hotel building, up four floors, or even a block away. These items are part of getting *into the minds* of what your customers want and how they will perceive your restaurant. A full lot of cars indirectly tell your guests the restaurant is always busy. An empty lot gives the perception no one is going to the restaurant. Again, their *perception* is part of your marketing.

REAL-LIFE STORY

The break-in that wasn't supposed to happen.

The first alarm sounded at 12:35 AM. After all, it was the perfect timing. The manager had just set the alarm, walked out, and locked the front door. She disappeared to the local watering hole and pulled up a chair to the bar. As soon as she sat down, she received the call from me. It went like this: "Mary, are you still at the restaurant?" She says, "No, I'm at the bar down the street." "Okay, I am receiving a security call from the security company, and they are telling me the alarm is going off. Can you run by the restaurant and see what is going on?" "Sure thing, I will call you when I get there."

Ten minutes went by, and my phone rang with Mary on the other end. I said, "The security company is telling me the back-glass door alarm is going off." So, Mary walks over to the door, looks it up and down, and opens and closes the door. "Nope, it isn't broken, and the door is closed." So, I said, "Please look around because it seems weird that the alarm is going off unless someone punched the glass and shook the windows or door." After walking around for ten minutes, Mary called back and said, "The place is secure, boss, and I'm setting the alarm and leaving." We thought that was the end of it.

Mary left, and within ten minutes of leaving the property, I received another security call. This time, it was from the same security person, and she said, "Your alarm is going off again, and to me, there must be something wrong with the system. Do you want me to cancel it?" I wondered why this would happen for a moment, and then I asked her the famous question I had asked many times before. "Are there any other sensors going off in the building?" "Nope, just that one area, and I think it's not a big deal, so I am going to cancel the alarm and reset it." So that's what she did. I went back to bed and wondered if that was the right thing to do instead of calling the police.

Thirty minutes later, the security person called again. She said, "Okay, I think I should send the police over there." "Why?" I asked. She replied, "Because now, every one of your sensors is going off, including the sensors in the bar, kitchen, office, and doorway." Immediately, I knew someone was in there. She called the police, and I called Mary back and said, "You have to meet the police at the restaurant because someone is in there."

Fifteen minutes later, Mary returns my call and says, "Okay, I am with the police, and they are walking the building with their guns drawn. Someone was in the restaurant, and they broke into the cash drawer at the bar, and then smashed open the office door, went upstairs, and broke into the safe. When I walked into the office area, there were checks placed on the floor in a circle, almost like the thieves were sitting in place counting items. The cash bags are gone too. Boss, whoever was in here surely knew what they were doing and knew what they were looking for."

The people were not caught, but they were brilliant. I am assuming this is what they did: They watched from the back window, and once the second alarm went off, they broke the glass and slipped through the glass door but did not open it. This was smart because if the door did not open, the alarm for that area would not go off, and it would appear no one was in the restaurant. Once inside, they could go into the office area and rest in place. Without any movement, this allowed the security company to reset the alarm. Once the alarm was reset, the thieves knew they could sit upstairs and do what they needed to do. Upstairs did not have any security, and why would it? It was on the second floor.

So, the final alarm went off as the thieves were *leaving the property*, not while they were entering it. Fuckers!!!

WORD OF MOUTH

****

3

This is one of the most critical aspects of creating buzz for your restaurant. *No buzz, no business*! Let's find out what gets your place buzzing.

WORD-OF-MOUTH MARKETING (WOM)

It has been said the best marketing is word-of-mouth marketing. But what is it? Word-of-mouth marketing is when one person verbally tells another person about a great experience they had at a restaurant. Then that person tells another, and it continues down the line until more and more people know about it. New restaurant news travels fast. So, it's up to you to get the word out.

HOW DOES IT HAPPEN?

Word of mouth marketing starts from the moment a lease is signed. Once it's signed, the marketing blitz should begin. So, do these steps:

- Tell your friends
- Call your relatives
- Knock on the doors of the building you are opening in and tell the tenants

- If it's a high-rise, ask to be in the building's newsletter
- Tell everyone you can
- Post your excitement on Facebook & Instagram
- Take a picture of yourself in front of the space and post it online
- Heck, do a little dance in front of it and post it on TikTok. (Maybe it will go viral)

To get this completed, the total cost would be **zero**. It's simply passing the information to one person and so on. This will create the "buzz" every new restaurant needs to get before opening. Lastly, post the info more than once. Post one in the morning and one in the late evening. (Schedule it every hour on Facebook pages.)

STEPS IN GETTING MORE WOM

- Once you find a location, send a tweet or social media post about the place you have found
- After the lease has been signed, send another tweet or social media post with a photo of you in front of the building or lease papers in hand
- Tag the editors of the local food-related blogs on IG, Twitter, etc.
- Hang a sign in the front of the building telling people you are opening soon
- Create a website and begin capturing emails for future marketing
- Create the Facebook, Google, Instagram page for the restaurant

- Once the architectural plans have been completed, start posting the renderings on your social media pages
- Once you open, always have a wait. Overbook if you have to. Waits indirectly tell people you are busy!
- Take photos of the construction and post the pictures, keeping people interested and continuing the word-of-mouth

MANAGEMENT TEAM

The management of a restaurant can make or break you in many ways. First, they can ruin your reputation and create negative word of mouth by treating the employees poorly. This happens because either the manager has not been appropriately trained or they do not have the experience to manage people. (They may even be old-school and think it's customary to yell at employees!)

Here is an example of a successful manager versus an unsuccessful manager: During service, the successful manager is *helping everyone* in all areas, and they are not directing others to do a job.

On the flip side, the unsuccessful manager stands around *directing, pointing, and telling* people to do their job. Again, this is an instant failure. I have seen it happen, and it only took one seasoned employee to walk up to me and say, "If that new manager tells me to bus a table again and he just stands there not helping, I am personally going to tell him to bus the fucking table himself!"

Hire and train the managers and ensure they work with everyone, rather than against everyone. The result will be positive word-of-mouth for all employees, and you will retain happy employees longer than your competitors.

DEMOGRAPHICS

By telling local or neighborhood people and magazines, the word will get passed along without you even knowing it. Why? Because people like to be in the "know." They want to spread the word and be the first to "know" about the rumored new restaurant/business coming in.

MARKETING MATERIAL

****

4

This part of the book talks about the branding of your company. Yes, you can do it yourself, but hire a pro to get it done if you are unsure. It will set your image and perception for your future guests. Dive in!

WEBSITE IMAGES

The images you use on the website will reflect your branding. Using professional photos will project a professional view of the company. If you do not have any pictures, stop by CANVA and sign up to use their website and graphics. You can find tons of pictures along with marketing material on their website. If you want to save some money, use images of the architect's pages first or even the architect's renderings. They work well and also give the reader some information about the design.

A note about the names of saved images. When the photos are saved & named, name them your business name and add a number 1, 2, 3, etc., after it. The reason is they will now become a searchable search engine result for images of your business name. It will also assist in leading people to your site by selecting the photo link. Keep in mind that Google's results are in the format of "all," "news," "images," "videos," and "shopping." The opportunity to be in many or all is up to you.

MARKETING COLLATERAL

There will also need some marketing collateral. Again, Canva is a great site to get the job done or try Vistaprint. Vistaprint is less expensive and faster than Canva, although Canva has many design options and beautiful shipping boxes! The one item here is to design it on Canva and then print it.

LOGO

The new business will need a logo. My favorite place to create a logo is FIVERR. It's a great site, and you can get a logo completed for as little as fifty dollars. Plus, they will send it back to you within two days. Once the logo has been completed, splash the logo on everything possible and begin marketing the brand. PS, ask for a transparent logo as well as a jpg image.

TO GO MENUS

While you may not have the final version of the menu, you can always print an example of the menu. The first thing a guest will ask you is, "What type of food will you be serving?" If you have a sample menu on your website, you will quickly see "that page" is the most viewed page. Hang a box from your front window and place some sample menus in the box. You will be surprised at how many people take a sample menu. Again, this is another form of marketing. You are feeding your future customers *information* and dripping it to them a little at a time.

QR CODES

A QR code will help you in many areas of marketing. The first way is to allow potential customers to see your menu. A simple scan with their handheld phone, and they are looking at your menu. The QR code should be printed on every piece of marketing collateral you offer. It's easier and faster than punching in a domain name. If you purchase the QR code generator on the app store, it will show how many people scanned the code. (Great tool) It's a great marketing tool to help you see essential data when and if the code gets used.

Some examples for a QR code would be to record three or four videos of the chef and post them on the restaurant's YOUTUBE channel. Then, if you have a QR code on the menu, the customers can scan the code, and the chef welcomes them to the restaurant.

BUSINESS CARDS

Boring - I agree. But how about if you use your QR code, print it on the cards, and link it to a hello video you created on Vimeo? Vimeo is easy, and the QR code is just as easy. Just connect the QR code to the Vimeo video, and you have an instant introduction. Better yet, place the QR code on your home page and have it linked to a YouTube or Vimeo video of the owner introducing themselves. Use your creativity, and you will get noticed.

BIT.LY (Mini URL)

Using a smaller URL will benefit you when using Twitter and/or the Instagram and Facebook pages. Keep in mind the reasoning for the tiny URL are the data "reports" you receive from using Bit.ly. It also reduces the number of characters you use on Twitter.

When logged into the Bit.ly app, it will report the number of times the shortened link was opened. This information is critical: It tells you what medium is working. For example, if you use a different Bit.ly code for each marketing piece, the reports will tell you where the people are opening the code.

HOW A BUSINESS MARKETS ITSELF

This is an area you can do by yourself. My favorite is constantcontact.com, and I have used it for over fifteen years. It's a drag-and-drop site, and you can collect and create an email database and even schedule the times for the email blast to be sent. There is another email marketing service called Mailchimp.com. These are excellent tools where restaurant owners can help themselves and reduce marketing dollars while increasing profits.

NEXTDOOR APP

While this app has been around, it appears to be getting more traction. This is an app that local residents can sign up under their neighborhood's house location. They log in and then prove they live in a respective house, and then they can go onto the site under their real name. It appears the site confirms the identity with the local tax assessor.

Either way, this site (appropriately used) works well with word-of-mouth marketing. But, remember this; It also works towards a business's disadvantage. If someone doesn't like service, they will post it quickly, and the entire neighborhood will know. So, it's crucial to monitor this site as the business owner of the restaurant and respond accordingly.

There are many avenues to use when marketing a business; you have to decide what area assists the company best.

YELP PHOTOS – LOCAL CUSTOMERS

Dare I even mention YELP. Hmmm, hard pass. Every person I know in the business cannot stand them. So that's all they get in the book.

TRIP ADVISOR – BUSINESS TRAVELERS

This is similar to the above. You can create an account in Trip Advisor and add the business images. The benefit here is the photos are ones *the business* has added, so you know they should be correct. PS, Trip Advisor is also great for businesspeople and is referred to in many European countries.

PRO-START SCHOOLS

Restaurants are always looking for staffing, so why not help yourself and invite the local Pro-Start kids in for a tour of the restaurant. It will allow the restaurant to market itself while also introducing the students to the restaurant. The end game here is that you may hire a few of these kids.

****

PUBLICIST STORY

Melissa Libby Associates – Thinkmla.com – Atlanta, Georgia, as told by Melissa Libby.

"When I was a young publicist working for a luxury hotel company in Atlanta, I picked up famed food writer John Mariani from the Atlanta airport. It was in July in a car with *no working air conditioning.* He was arriving to review Opus, the hotel's restaurant I was working with. Thirty years later, we still laugh about that day.

Working with John over the years, learning his preferences, and passing them along to my client's restaurants, has resulted in much coverage from him, probably most notably when The Optimist was named Best New Restaurant in the Country by Esquire magazine.

John is a very likable person, and it was my pleasure to spend time getting to know him to the benefit of my clients. Good thing he didn't hold that first, very sweaty ride against me!"

WEBSITE

****

5

A website is a massive part of your branding and marketing. This section talks about why it's so important and how you can use it to your advantage. Here we go.

GETTING STARTED

Here are the steps in getting a website up and "live."

- Secure a domain name on GoDaddy or another domain registrar
- Create a website on either Weebly or Wix
- Join the Canva app and use their pictures for the website, and name every image differently
- Link your website to your domain name
- Use descriptive words for the META tags title
- Publish the website, and wham, it's online

SEARCH ENGINE OPTIMIZATION

Google is the largest search engine, so it's crucial to take advantage of its dominance.

Knowing how to get your site in the search engines and maintain search result relevance is very important. Here are some tips:

- Submit your website to the search engines via Google My Business Profile Manager
- Add different keywords to every page, so the META TAGS are relevant to your business
- Keep your website updated weekly with blog posts

- Add a site map to your site pages

- Add the Google My Business analytic code to your website footer and have Google crawl the site. The site will walk you through the steps

- Be sure to name each page differently, so the search engines crawl and recognize different words

- Ensure every page, title, keyword, and description is different. The result will be better search results positioning.

****

THOUGHTS TO PONDER – (Search engines)

Searching for specific terms on different devices may yield different results. For example, handheld devices show one item, and other devices may show others.

Another item here is the number of times you pitch a story. Keep a log of the stories pitched to writers, and you will quickly see the more times you pitch an idea, the better the odds of being featured.

****

Here's a search result example of the best seafood restaurant in the United States.

WEBSITE ANALYTICS * (See the example)

When people talk about marketing, they are typically talking about something intangible. In this section, I review the tangible and deemed essential marketing data. It's not *advertising*. Always pass on the traditional advertising. *It does not work!* This section includes website setup & visits, email statistics, email opening rate, and social media analytics.

The website analytics includes the number of visits, pages visited, referral pages, visitors' time on the website, and the keywords searched. This information is critical in analyzing marketing.

The business owner or manager will need to log into the server hosting the website to review this information. Within the website's back-end software are the facts and data to analyze. This can determine if the marketing efforts are working. Within the website's statistical pages may be the referral pages of where the visitors are coming from. This may include search engines like Google, BING, Duck Duck Go, Yahoo, or even social media pages like Instagram or Facebook. It may even include pages from news sites that may have written about your business.

*WEBSITE ANALYTICS EXAMPLE

Note the difference from *unique* views to *page* views on the next page graphic. "Unique" is *one* person visiting the site several times but counts as *one visit*. As seen below, the average person visits 1.21 pages. It doesn't show the length of time on the site, but, on average, it's less than a minute.

****

EXAMPLE OF A TITLE & META TAGS

Meta tags are in the source code of the web pages. (Source codes create the pages.) They (The words) are used in search engine results. To see them on your or your competitor's pages that are higher than yours in search results, right-click their webpage and select "view source."

This is the page title:
<title>**Hungry Hospitality - Hungry Hospitality - Restaurant Consulting - Atlanta**</title>

This is the META page description:
<meta property="og:description" content="**Hungry Hospitality - Restaurant Consultants**" />

This is the META keywords for the search engine:
<meta name="keywords" content="**restaurant consultants, hungry hospitality, restaurant advisors, business consultants, assessments, hotel advisors, business advisors,**"/>

If you use Weebly or Wix as a website creator, there will be an area explaining how to complete the web pages' titles and descriptions.

WEBSITE TOOLS

The business owner or manager will need to log into the server hosting the website to review this information. Within the website's back-end software are the facts and reports to analyze, which can determine if the marketing efforts are working or not. The website's statistical pages are the referral pages of where the visitors are coming from. This may include search engines like Google or Yahoo or even social media pages like Instagram or Facebook. It may even include pages from news sites that may have written about your business.

The website analytics includes the number of visits to the website, the number of pages visited on the website, the website visitors are being referred from, the length of time visitors are on your website, and the keywords referring the visitors to your website. All of this information is critical in analyzing marketing.

Why is this important? It will report how the customers are finding out about the business. Want to know when the business name is being mentioned online? Search for Google alerts and add the company name to the alert section. It's free, and anytime the company is mentioned in an online search, an email will be sent to the account's email address. It's an excellent tool to find out about the news on the company or *competitors*. Use it wisely.

****

SEARCHING FOR MEDIA TOPICS – *New school*

There are two media service companies that help in locating upcoming stories. One is **CISION,** and the other is called **MUCKRACK**. (Newest) These are the single most important "media generators." They are media databases filled with editors, writers, freelance journalists and dates of upcoming articles, searchable topics, and contacts information. This is where you become steps ahead of your competition and the number one reason you should hire a publicist. Why? Most publicists have a subscription to this service. Order it yourself, and the service costs range from $3000-$5000 annually. Plus, your time gets sucked away! Examples of how Cision works: You can search by the writer's topic, the writer's name, and the result will show their recent articles. The searchable results will help in their pitches to writers. You can also build media databases.

Now, you may be thinking, I can do this. You may be correct. Personally, I have tried. I did great at it but being a business owner means wearing many hats. Marketing is a full-time job requiring everyday attention. If you begin looking into either of these, it may become a detraction to your real job. Let the pros do it for you.

How do you get noticed by the writers in these services? Write something interesting the editor's readers will be interested in reading. Maybe write a pitch about how your business can help others. Either way, write a story about something different. The more boring you are, the more times the pitch will be ignored. Oh, and don't blame the publicist. Even though they will be pitching stories, the business owner should be the one helping the publicist. If you do not help them and feed editors juicy information, they may pitch your restaurant to a writer on the quarterly new root vegetable available on the menu. How fuckin boring. **Get creative and get recognized!**

****

PUBLICIST STORY – As told by the author, Clifford Bramble – Hungry Hospitality LLC

When the Magazine food critic arrived at the restaurant, she was shown a table inside the restaurant. She politely declined and asked to be seated outside on the patio. I freaked. Here's why.

An hour before her arrival, I was at Home Depot buying silicone caulking. The caulking was to seal the grease traps situated directly below the patio tables. Grease traps are where the kitchen's wastewater goes, emitting sewer-type gas smells. Since it was in June, the grease traps were emitting fumes all week, and I tried to solve the scent with various ideas. Fortunately, the caulking worked, and without knowing, the food critic requested a table directly on top of the grease traps. Nothing was ever said, so we figured that she did not smell anything.

PRE-OPENING MARKETING

****

6

Planning the opening of a restaurant takes a lot of thought and a lot of planning. My view is there should be at least a six-month time frame to plan for the marketing and opening of a restaurant. If done correctly, the results will be excellent. In this section, we review areas that can help in the pre-opening. Giddy up.

CREATING YOUR STORY

Before opening, publicists will assist you in creating and telling your story. This will generate curiosity and may keep people talking about the upcoming opening. This is a high priority for everyone.

BRAND RECOGNITION

By talking about the new restaurant, you are creating a new brand. By making the brand, you are creating a new image. So, the more the restaurant can get mentioned before opening, the more people will talk about it.

WORD-OF-MOUTH MARKETING

As mentioned in a previous lesson, word-of-mouth marketing will help you before and after opening. However, getting the word-of-mouth marketing going before the restaurant opens supports the after-opening marketing.

FINDING FUTURE ARTICLES

Suppose the marketing person can get ahold of the calendars for a local, regional, or national magazine or Internet sites that write about products like yours. In that case, it will give you the upper hand at getting this information out to the editors. If they have the information in a press release form, they may look at it and include it within their articles. MUCKRACK does a great job of this type of competitor analysis. One of their reports can show the number of articles you have received compared to a competitor. If your competitor gets all the media, you should start contacting the writer, hoping they write about you.

ESTABLISHING A BRAND

Before opening, the new restaurant's name should begin to be promoted. The goal is to market the business as much as possible *before it opens*, so customers will think you have *already opened*. If you wait until the restaurant opens, the marketing will already be behind in its promotions.

ANNUAL ROUND-UPS

Each year, food writers and editors write an annual roundup of what is happening or what is about to occur for restaurants. If you have the contact information of the writers or editors writing these articles, and you can get information to them three to six months in advance, it would be great to get included in the write-up. The more times the restaurant name is mentioned, the better name brand recognition the restaurant will gain.

THOUGHT TO PONDER:

- If you think people do not know where you are and that adding blinking lights to the exterior will help, it won't
- An empty parking lot reflects poorly on the restaurant and creates negative word of mouth

- Placing a new OPEN sign in the front window. It's a killer for business
- No lights around the parking lot. It creates a dark and closed-looking atmosphere
- Continuously placing help wanted ads in the online hiring boards. It shows lots of turnover and creates the why are they always hiring question (Pre-Covid)

SEARCHING FOR COMPETITORS

Why would you do this? It's not what you are searching for that is essential. It's the results. For example, if you search for a competitor, the results may show every article written about the competitor. This is important because a writer or editor writes the articles. BINGO. You now have the contact for the story and now have the opportunity to contact the writers. Be creative and use the Internet to work for you!

How do you find the contacts? Go to Twitter or LinkedIn and search for their name. It's a simple thing to do. Push yourself to get it done rather than waiting for them to call you. Go – Try it now!

LOCAL MONTHLY PUBLICATIONS

Monthly publications plan at least three months in advance. So, if you want to provide information to be printed for their December issue, it's best to send it to them by September. Some magazines plan six months out. The most important item here is knowing who to send the information to. If you have the editor's email or information, they should be receiving the information as soon as you can. As mentioned previously, this information can be retrieved from their websites, book mastheads, MuckRack, or Cision.

QUARTERLY PRINT MAGAZINES

Similar to the above, but these magazines are printed quarterly. They still need content, so it may as well be yours, right? Please plan accordingly and send them the information several months before the print date.

DAILY WEB ARTICLES NEEDED

Obviously, the Internet pages and sites need new content to stay relevant. This information can be sent to the writers daily, and hopefully, your business will be mentioned. Think about this: A daily site needs new information *daily*. Without it, they cannot provide their readers with new information. *That's a lot of new information.* Hopefully, the more relevant pitches that get sent to the writer, the more they will consider the pitch.

ANNUAL PUBLICATIONS

The regional and national publications plan at least six months before the issue, as with local monthly publications. So please plan and send them the information at the right time.

****

THOUGHT TO PONDER #1

You will never get more press than you receive before or immediately after opening a restaurant. If the reviews are all excellent, the articles may continue. However, if the reviews are poor, it could put the restaurant out of business faster than one thinks.

THOUGHT TO PONDER #2

When one editor sees a new restaurant has just been written about, they may want to write about it too. Everybody wants to be the first to talk about a new restaurant opening, but sometimes it doesn't happen. So, they will still write about it to be relevant and show they are aware of the latest happenings on the scene. It never hurts to email the article to other writers. It may pique their interest and write a story based upon a different pitch/angle.

****

REMEMBER THIS: A person once asked me, "Who does that restaurant groups PR?" My reply was, "They do it internally, why do you ask?" The response was interesting. "I ask because they sure get a lot of press." My reply was simple. "They get a lot of press because they always do **something different and continue to open restaurants**. Of course, they get a lot of press."

*It's when one rests on their laurels; they become **irrelevant**.*

****

PRE-OPENING 3 MONTHS OUT

****

7

After reading the last chapter, you may have thought that is pretty easy. But, don't get so comfortable. Marketing never stops. When it does, business stops! Let's go!

IS THE MEDIA KIT READY?

By now, your media kit should be completed and saved as a pdf. Additionally, the press releases, press photos, menus, and fact sheets should be completed. Finally, if you are a tech-savvy person, you should have a Google room or private docsend folder available for writers to locate the information. The nice part of a docsend folder is you can control who sees it and when they access it. You can also change the information within it at your leisure.

CONSTRUCTION UPDATES

Another item to keep your customers updated on is the construction progress. Again, this creates excellent word-of-mouth marketing opportunities for the business and keeps you in their mind. Part of this communication with your guests will be photos of the construction, upcoming dates to remember, and the expected opening date.

FURNITURE & FIXTURES

Every time a new piece of equipment or furniture goes into the building and is set in place, the business has a unique photo opportunity. If the photos are used as a tool, this will keep the restaurant in their mind. Remember, people always want to be the first to "know" about something, and posting new information about the furniture or equipment keeps those same people in the know!

HOST A TASTING MENU WITH LOCALS

People love, love, love to be part of tasting the new menu. Just try it. Invite twenty people in for a pre-opening menu tasting and see how many people show up. This is an excellent avenue to keep customers engaged with your marketing. Ultimately, they will continue to tell others about the status of the opening.

PRE-OPENING FRONT ENTRANCE EVENT

Piggybacking on the previous note, if the restaurant is located on a busy street, and people drive by daily, once they see a tent or something going on in the lot, they will begin to wonder what is happening. But, again, this is all part of the psychology of your marketing. So, keep your future customers engaged and wondering when the restaurant will be opening or what is happening there.

MEET & GREET WITH THE CHEF

Here is another inexpensive way to meet the local customers. Invite fifty people in for a "meet the chef" happy hour. The restaurant doesn't even have to be open. The goal is to invite the customers in and meet the players. The customers, in turn, will tell many of their friends they were invited to a new restaurant opening and met the chef. Remember, it's easy to sit on your hands and do nothing, but opening a new restaurant is anything but that. Be different and stay exciting.

CONSTRUCTION TOUR

Another excellent idea to keep word-of-mouth marketing going: Once areas of the restaurant are safe to enter, invite fifty or so people in for a construction "hard hat tour." Hand out the hard hats, bring the guests into the space, and give them a tour. Keep in mind many people may have never been in a commercial kitchen, so this will be an excellent opportunity to see something different. This simple fifteen or twenty-minute tour will get many people excited, and it does not cost a dime. It keeps people engaged!

PRESS TOUR AND TASTING

This has been mentioned several times, but opening a restaurant can generate lots of media coverage. The question is, how does the media get the information to cover the event? One way is to invite the press and host a press party.

While this can generate excellent coverage, be sure the restaurant is ready.

So, what is a press party? The press party is an invite-only party where the media is invited for a tour and tasting on the new menu. This can be good for food writers, bloggers, influencers, or even the local neighborhoods. The goal is to get them into the restaurant and show them the entire operation. Hopefully, they will be the first to see and report on the space.

There are risks involved too. If the service or food is not excellent, one can risk receiving poor press coverage. The press party option is available and should be thought about and discussed thoroughly before completing this event. Finally, a publicist can provide valuable insight into this opportunity.

REAL-LIFE STORY

****

Who in their right mind wants to open a restaurant in the worst part of town, on the backside of the railroad tracks, and in an area where the prostitutes are still on the sidewalk at eight o'clock on a Sunday morning? You are about to find out.

At one of the restaurants I co-founded, this was precisely the issue. What started as a negative to the business ended up being the best marketing tool ever. What was the tool? It was word-of-mouth. The best kind of marketing a brand can have, and it was turned into the coolest destination location ever.

The restaurant was in a bad part of town, and there was not a streetlight to be found. The main reason was they were all shot out *with guns*. So picture this. A Lambo was driving down a totally dark street, driving past the public housing units, and stopping directly in front of the "no street solicitation sign." With people standing on the street, admiring the car, if I were the driver, I would be wondering, "Where the hell is this place?" But Lambo after Lambo and then the Bentleys, and the Ferrari's and the high-end Benzes all arrived and had to drive down the same dark streets.

What was the cool part of this? The cool part was the high-end cars and customers alike had to drive from the suburbs to this out-of-the-way destination restaurant. While driving down the dark streets, they had to find the restaurant. First, since there wasn't any restaurant sign, they had to guess they were going into the correct lot. Then, all they had to do was locate the valet parking. Once they found them, they felt safe.

This alone created anticipation on so many levels, and along with it came the cool factor and word-of-mouth for the restaurant. These people helped create word-of-mouth or the "What the hell are you thinking?" or the "I had to drive through the hood to get here." It was the best marketing ever, and as more and more high-end cars drove through the "hood," it only got busier and busier. So keep in mind: Use your surroundings as a marketing tool.

****

HOW CELEBRITIES HELP WITH MARKETING

When it comes to your guests, you may be in an area that never sees any celebrities, or if you are in Atlanta, they may be everywhere. Here's an example: In some of the restaurants I co-owned, celebrities like LeAnn Rimes, Jennifer Lawrence, Billy Crystal, Bette Midler, Betty White, Elton John, Will Farrell, Jacque Pepin, Cam Newton, Matt Ryan, Tyler Perry, Ben Stiller, Hall & Oats, Demi Moore, Ashton Kutcher, Ian Somerhalder, Nina Dobrev, Keifer Sutherland, Jennifer Nettles, Marisa Tomei, Woody Harrelson, Usher, Oprah Winfrey, and so many more dined in the restaurant. The NFL owners even dined in the restaurant.

So, when a celebrity enters the restaurant and the other guests see them dining, the buzz goes across the restaurant rapidly. Then, the buzz continues via social media, and it's a viral effect that helps with word-of-mouth. Sometimes, it gets into the local news or online publications. Either way, it's another area of credibility for the restaurant when someone famous walks into your restaurant.

OPENING WEEK

If everything has been appropriately planned and the mock service and trial runs have been completed successfully, the first day should be a breeze. If not, it could be a disaster. So, what should be done to make it a success?

A week before opening, there should be scheduled role-plays & trial runs for the kitchen and the service areas. This may include serving guests (but no media), ensuring the staff has the menu items cooked correctly, and the service staff are ready.

Keep in mind there are a million little steps to make a successful first-week opening. Some of these steps include: Setting up the POS system correctly, having the recipe cards available, the menu set up correctly, and ensuring the service staff knows how to ring in the orders. The trial runs should go off easily by guaranteeing these items have been checked off. Plus, the customers in for the test runs will enjoy their meals.

More importantly, is the media coverage. Use every day of trial service or the opening week as an opportunity to post items on your social media pages. You lose a great chance to keep people in the know if you do not.

Lastly, the media kits can go out at your leisure rather than when you are not ready. Be sure the BOH and FOH staff are ready, and only then should the press kits go out to the media.

ALREADY OPEN

****

8

By far, this will be one of the hardest things to do. The reason is simple. After being open for a while, most people may have tried the restaurant once and may have made up their minds. They either love it, or they don't. So, get your big boy/girl pants on because this will take a lot of work. Here we go.

IS THE RESTAURANT ALREADY OPEN?

If you have a business that has been open for a while, and you are just beginning to market it, you will need to develop something pretty good and *different* to get a writer's attention. The reason, as mentioned before, is the restaurant will **get the most press when it first opens**.

If the press is excellent, the media coverage may continue to be written. After that, it will be up to you to feed the editors and writers with new and innovative information. FYI, these days, a menu change will not be enough.

A new chef could be it, but if it's a chef change, begin to invite as many writers and editors as possible in for press parties and treat it as an opening.

WHY IT'S HARD TO MARKET RESTAURANTS ALREADY OPEN

The number one reason is *perception*. Because the restaurant is already open, the perception by the local diners and writers has already been decided. This means they either think the restaurant is excellent, too pricey, have great or poor service, and customers have already decided their *feelings* towards the restaurant. Feelings are important!

Another reason is the restaurant has already either received excellent or poor articles written about them, and there is nothing to change the customer's minds. So, the editors are looking for something different that will pique their readers' interest.

CHANGES

If the restaurant has been open, and there haven't been any significant changes, more than likely, no editor or writer will be interested in writing about the restaurant. But, being different can create an exciting article. So, the challenge here is being different and standing out in the crowd?

WHAT CAN YOU DO?

A few items to think about. Is it busy, and do you need a publicist? Skip this step if the restaurant is busy making a profit and operating on autopilot. Also, if a business has slowed down over time, it may be time to try the following.

First, change the chef or change the menu to an entirely new menu. Anytime there is a change of a chef and or food, it interests the guests, writers and, editors. It piques their interest, but will it be enough to get them in to try the new menu? If you select this option, plan on a huge marketing plan around this change.

Second. Remodel the interior. If the restaurant is dated, it may be time to update the place and look new again. Again, this will get people talking and will create word of mouth. Sometimes a change of paint color will help! There is also a restaurant in Nashville that changes chefs every two years. Again, this keeps it fresh and maintains interest.

Third. Create an annual event and make it huge. I mean big. Tie it to a local school and donate a portion of the profits to the school. The nice part about this is the event should become an annual *community event*. After all, you are creating *lasting memories.*

If any one of these is done, it will be time to invite people to try and tour the new place. This includes food editors, bloggers, influencers, and your local VIPs.

This all comes with lots of planning and a considerable cost. However, an old, not-so-busy restaurant can become the new hip spot if promoted correctly. It involves proper planning and execution.

****
REAL-LIFE STORY

Over the past twenty-five years, I have accumulated a database of editors, writers, and publishers' emails and phone numbers. I always figured these numbers would be invaluable and needed at one point in my career. So, when it was time to contact a national writer in a major magazine, this is how it went.

On the second ring, the person answered. Amazingly, it was a direct number to their cell phone. The call was fast and straightforward. "Hi, we are opening a new restaurant and would like to invite you in to see it. Will you be in Palm Desert anytime soon?" The answer was quick. "Why, as a matter of fact, I will be in the area next Thursday night. I would love to stop by and dine. Can you reserve a table for me at 7:00 PM for three people? Please know this will be a complete review of your restaurant." Astonished and excited, and after some small talk, the call ended.

Over the next week, I was doing my homework on what to expect from this person. I knew we would be ready, and the result could help nationally.

Fast forward to the following week, and it was a Wednesday night. The restaurant was packed, and there were no open tables available. The bar was standing room only, and servers were running around taking care of their guests. The reviewer walked into the restaurant and directly to the host area without warning. "Hi, my name is Rainy, and I am here for my 7:00 reservation." The host peered into the laptop and did not know the person or see the person's name, so he asked the reviewer for their name again. Again, the host looked into the computer and remember this was a national restaurant reviewer, and the host looked up and said, "I'm sorry, but you do not have a reservation, and we are filled for the evening." That was the beginning of a bad night.

The reviewer looked around and spotted someone she knew and said, "I think you better show my business card to that woman over there." So, the host walked over to the person the reviewer was talking about and handed her the business card, and said, "This person upfront says she has a reservation tonight and she is not in the reservation system. She seems a bit pushy to me, and I have never heard of her." The person didn't even have to look to know who it was but what she did know was the reviewer was in the house. All the person said was, "Find a table for the reviewer fast and with no excuses." The host replied, "I am out of tables, and we have a bunch of reservations arriving." Without hesitation, the person said, "Find a table, and the other guests will have to wait."

The reviewer was seated within a ten-minute time frame, but the dinner and service were not what the reviewer had expected, and the entire evening kept going down. First, the drinks and food began getting sent back. Then, it was the wrong drink and, the salad was overdressed. Lastly, the proteins were sent back as being overcooked. It was ugly! Needless to say, the review never came out, and the excitement with the opportunity to have a significant review was ruined.

So, while the marketing contact was called and did walk in and dine at the restaurant, while we thought we were ready to serve the reviewer, either we got the day wrong, or the reviewer arrived and surprised us the night before. Either way, we were not ready. It was a clusterfuck!

ONGOING MARKETING

****

9

The daily marketing by a restaurant should be part of the management crew's responsibility. If not, they should have someone on board responsible for doing their social media daily. This daily responsibility includes:

- At least five scheduled and timed out posts on the restaurant's Facebook Page
- Five "shares" of the same post by each member of the staff (For maximum view)
- Five posts on Instagram along with tags of editors or food writers
- Five business-related posts on LinkedIn along with a link to the menu page of the restaurant
- Five posts on their Google Business page along with links to the webpage
- A weekly or twice monthly email blast to their patrons, which should include at least five links to be tracked
- One food-related *article* written by a member of the staff and posted on the LinkedIn creator page

As one can see, the more the restaurant gets marketed, the more brand recognition becomes easily recognized. It's the responsibility of the business leaders to ensure items like the above occur. If not, the restaurant will become just like the others that are not receiving any new press.

SALON'S & LOCAL SPA'S

What is the big deal here, right? The big deal is that the technician, or salons, will be spending thirty to sixty minutes of quality time with the locals in these types of places. They talk about everything! Why not let them tell their clients about your restaurant? Also, telling the local salons, nail salons, and spas you are opening a restaurant or already have one will give them something to talk to their customers about.

HANDOUTS

As part of your word-of-mouth marketing, you should have some free cards or drink cards to hand out to these people. They will either use them or hand the cards out to their customers.

DAILY MARKETING

Daily blogs, restaurant sites, and hospitality sites require new information every day.

The editors are looking for information to write about. Why can't it be you? It can, but you have to provide the information to the editors. You or a publicist have to be the one coming up with creative headlines or events. For the daily areas, Facebook, Instagram, Eater.com, & The Daily Meal, are a few that come to mind that you can market to. Facebook and Instagram are free, and you should use them as much as possible. Eater.com is an online restaurant site based on a city-by-city basis. (Keep in mind who the *readers* are on these sites.)

WEEKLY

Along with the daily blogs, plenty of weekly and monthly blogs and articles are being written. As a restaurateur, it's your responsibility to either get the articles written about you or hire a publicist to do so. Hiring a publicist will probably set you back a good $2000.00 a month with a six-month retainer. However, if you choose to do this yourself, you may become a creative genius operating a restaurant.

MONTHLY

Similar to the weekly articles or postings, monthly articles are also needed. These articles will need at least three or even six-month lead time. Again, it's up to you to figure a way to get the articles written about your restaurant. If not a solo article, try to piggyback with others doing similar events like yours.

Here are a few ideas to consider:

- Monthly wine tastings
- Steak festivals to promote steak on the menu
- Summer lobster events
- Fall apple ingredient events
- Inclusion of local festivals where other chefs/restaurants will be involved

QUARTERLIES

Like the seasons, most quarterlies need information about restaurants and new products to interest their readers. But, as I have said previously, it's up to you to consider these opportunities and then present them with exciting material.

ANNUAL WRITE-UPS

The annual write-ups may include the best restaurants issue or the top chef issues. Either way, the writers are looking for interesting information to get into their posts. So please do your homework and find the best people to contact and send them information.

Here are a few ideas:

- A once a year event that will become an annual tradition by the locals
- An annual holiday event
- Annual cooking classes
- A once a year charity event for a local school
- Involvement by the restaurant in a yearly hospitality charity event or sponsorship of a high school student

EMPLOYEE MARKETING

One of the best areas to help you with your customers is your employees. Treat them well, respect them, and ensure they are making money, and they will be your best in-house marketing. They will pass on the good word to every customer, and your guests will return monthly.

■■

BEING PROACTIVE WITH REVIEWERS

There was a time when I had photos of every local, regional, and national restaurant reviewer. The pictures were posted on a wall in the kitchen, so the entire staff knew what the reviewers looked like. The goal was simple: If a restaurant reviewer walked into the restaurant, they would be recognized. There was even a bounty on their head!

****

MARKETING TO COMPETITORS

****

10

Whenever a new restaurant is opening, people begin to talk. One area that talks faster than others is in the competitor base. *Ignore them, and they may trample you.* Watch them, and you can learn from them. Do the latter and beat them at their own game!

HOW COMPETITORS CAN HELP YOU

No, you are not reading incorrectly. Before a restaurant opens, the first ones to know about it are typically the competition within a mile radius. So, use them to help you spread the word. How?

INTRODUCE YOURSELF

It's always a good idea to stop by and say hello to the management team and introduce yourself as the person in the restaurant next door. The reason is those competitors will be able to answer their own guest's questions when they are asked about "What is going on next door?" It shows they are in the know, and everyone wants to be in the know!

While introducing yourself, you can also get a glimpse of how their restaurant is doing at specific times of the day. For example, go to the restaurant one day at five o'clock and then again on a different day at nine o'clock. This will give you valuable information on when the locals are dining. As usual, the good and busy times will always be 6:30-8:30, depending on the location.

On the other hand, if the restaurant is in urban areas, the busy times may be 7:30-9:30. Either way, taking a visit to the competitor will be good for you to recognize the age of the diners, the attire of the diners, and the times they are eating.

WATCH THEIR PARKING LOTS

I would bet every time you drive by a restaurant and see the lot filled with cars, you think to yourself, "Wow, that place is always packed!" What about if the lot was empty? I bet you would be saying, "How does that place stay open, I never see any cars in their lot." First of all, what time are you driving by, but secondly, the perception you have in your mind is they are not busy. That would be considered to be poor word-of-mouth marketing. See, this is what a restaurant has to contend with; It's like learning to understand the psychology of the diners.

HAVE A DRINK AT THEIR BAR

Most bars have a great local clientele. If the restaurant you are opening is not in a downtown area, this will help you. When you sit at a local bar and meet local people, especially if you tell them you are opening a new restaurant, their eyes will light up and immediately say, "Where and what type of food will you be serving?" They will help you spread the word through good old word-of-mouth marketing.

****

MUSIC & MARKETING

Here is a fast thought to ponder. A restaurant's music directly affects the perception of the atmosphere. Play sleepy, slow music, and it's boring. Play slow jazz, and it feels upscale. And if you play pop, you will get another perception. So, based upon the menu, the furniture, fixture, and the staff's attire, play the correct music for the guests, and do not worry about what the employees say about it. The music is not for them. It's for the guests.

****

SOCIAL MEDIA

****

11

SOCIAL MEDIA PAGES

Social media is an excellent avenue to contact customers and become more familiar with them. So, let's take a look at a few more opportunities for free marketing.

GOOGLE MY BUSINESS

The easiest way to get included in Google My Business is to sign up with the <u>Google my business pages</u> and verify you are the site owner. Once the site is verified, the site will be crawled and spidered nightly. This means the business website will be added to the search engine and scanned nightly.

GETTING VERIFIED ON GOOGLE

The Google my business pages will present a code to you. It may be mailed to you, or sometimes, they will send a text with a code. Once you receive the code, you can complete the Google business page and be the verified owner of the page.

GOOGLE STATS

Several areas tell you the site traffic within the My Google Business page. The *"insights"* link is one of them. This one is important because it will show you the number of people searching the "name" of your business compared to the number of people finding your business through the search results. Another area shows you the results of the number of people that viewed your photos. Search around, and you will see the information is valuable for marketing.

Another option is the analytics of the **Google Business page**. This code should be copied and pasted into the website "footer" page, and then the website should be "published" again. Once it's published, you will return to the Google pages and tell them you have added the code. Their website will immediately crawl the website URL you punched in, and within two minutes, there will be a pop-up screen stating the website domain has been verified. On the other hand, the code may be mailed to you, and once you receive the card, you punch in the code and become the verified owner of the Google business account.

Lastly, one of the most critical areas to watch is the **Google review link**. Be sure to sign up on the link that will send you an email every time a review is posted.

SEARCHING FOR YOUR COMPANY NAME

Go to the Google search engine and punch in your website's domain name. So, if the domain name is www.coursini.com, punch it in and select enter. Any results with that specific domain name will show in the search results. If you do not see your domain name in the results, give it 24 hours and search for it again.

GOOGLE TRENDS

Google trends can be used strategically for yourself or your competitors to learn what people are currently searching for on Google. This is a perfect area to see where your company or any products you sell similar to others show up in the name results. It's also an excellent way to discover searched words to incorporate into your website content, thus increasing traffic within your website.

The goal for a small business is to use every opportunity to market themselves and in a frugal way. www.google.com/trends

GOING TIK-TOK-IN

When there is an opportunity for free marketing and brand awareness, people will find a way to use it to its advantage. This is what Tik Tok does. First, it's an opportunity to use it as a one-minute promotion. Yes, the demographics may not fit your company, but posting some funny clips about your products may help with marketing. You never know unless you try it, plus there are a million restaurant stories one can tell.

VIRTUAL INFLUENCERS

There are several new companies at the forefront of virtual media influencers. One is called <u>Offbeat Media Group,</u> and they are out of Atlanta. While this is not a free avenue for free marketing, it's a new type of marketing and undoubtedly one to watch.

SOCIAL MEDIA PAGES

If you are not using the free social media options, you should start immediately. It's another option to maintain and communicate with your customers.

For example, Facebook will allow visitors to "like" and "follow" the business page. It also lets the business owner to develop a following. It's an excellent way to keep in close contact with guests and become more familiar with them.

Facebook's Creator Studio for business is a perfect page to utilize too. Facebook Pages API allows you to "schedule" posts. In addition, Facebook's "live" feature will enable you to stream "live" options. On Instagram, the photos a company adds to its page will either be liked or not. You can even post a "story," a "reel," or video and keep it on your page for an extended time.

Everybody loves pictures, and it's now possible to post funny short videos, so post and tag as many people as possible: tag editors, newsrooms, and social media influencers. One never knows what may bring in a new customer.

Also, be sure to use the same name to set up the Instagram, Facebook, TikTok, and LinkedIn pages. It maintains the consistency of your brand. It would also benefit you to announce you have a page on each of your social media pages on the other social media. So, for instance, promote the Facebook page on Instagram and announce the Instagram page on Google business. The more you post on these areas, the more people will follow you.

One last item: If there is a marketing video available or someone in the company was featured in a podcast, television spot, or another type of video, it would be a good idea to screen record the video and edit it to one-minute portions. Then, use those one-minute portions to post on your IG or FB story. Don't forget to give credit to the person who created the video.

BLOGGERS/INFLUENCERS

Bloggers are the same as the above item. Search through either Twitter or Instagram, and you will find thousands of bloggers. Tag them and send them information.

PODCASTS

This is another area where a business can get some good press. There are many food and beverage podcasts out there that are always in need of having someone on their show. So be the person on the show and promote the show on your social media pages.

THE POWER OF YOUTUBE

Used correctly, YouTube can be an excellent marketing tool. Currently, it's one of the most-watched sites for younger kids. Once the account has been created, you can upload videos. These videos can be as little as two-minute bites of information to help others. An idea would be to record the chef creating several menu items. Split it into three or four small videos and upload them to your page. Using the search terms for YouTube, you may end up getting quite a following. The key is to be creative and make the videos public so everyone can see them. Then, on your profile, add the restaurant's website.

LIVE STREAMING SERVICE

This may not be for everyone but do it consistently and weekly to keep people's attention. An example is to use a service like Streamyard and connect it to every one of your social media pages. The service allows you to add destinations to stream your live webcast. It's an easy way to gain new followers, and as a chef or a manager, you always have new material. Being different is how you get noticed, and this is a perfect opportunity to be different.

****

REAL-LIFE STORY

In the restaurant business, finding employees has always been a challenge. This time, we found a new employee whose position was a dishwasher. This was the first day I dealt with the person.

Upon arrival, I saw a man sitting on the patio table. He was covered with tattoos from his face to the tips of his fingers. I looked at him and said, can I help you with something." His immediate reply startled me. He said, "Yea, you can go find that fucking asshole who hired me and tell him he needs to start paying me, or I'm going to kick his ass." I immediately knew this was a bad hire!

I walked into the restaurant and saw the manager who hired him and said, "There is some gang member out on the patio table, and he is telling me you hired him, and if he doesn't start work, he is going to kick your ass." I half laughed while telling him. The first impression was not good, but the issue was resolved, and interestingly enough, the man started working in the restaurant.

Over the next few weeks, every time the man was asked to do something or clean an area, his response was always the same. "I will get it done when I have a mother fucking minute." It became a comedy show, but after so many times, I had had enough, so I told the manager, "The person you hired has to go. He is disrespectful, yells swear words at the management, and seems like he will get in a fight with someone. I believe the staff is afraid of him." So, the decision was made that day. I said, "When he arrives, I will go up to him along with a witness and tell him he has been terminated."

At two o'clock that afternoon, the man walked in and went to punch in for his shift. I brought my witness with me, really as part protection, but I approached the individual and said, "Can I get a minute of your time?" He looked at me and said, "What the fuck do you want?" So, nicely, I said, "Yesterday was your last day working here, and we will not need your services any longer, so please go get your belongings out of the locker and leave the property."

The response was exactly what I expected. He squared off with me, face to face, and said, "I ain't going nowhere, and you can't fire me." When I say he was in my face, it was that close. So, I did the only thing I thought would get his attention. I looked at him and, as loud as I could yell, said, "LISTEN, MOTHER FUCKER, I'm not afraid of you. You have two minutes to get your belongings, and I am calling the police." His response was, 'I ain't afraid of no mother fucking police." So, I yelled to the hostess, "CALL 911 and get the police over here and tell them we have a trespasser on the property." I never saw a man move so fast. He was gone within those two minutes.

While it was a dangerous thing to do (yelling back), the manager with me started laughing and said, "Wow, I have never seen you like that before!" We both chuckled while the employee ran past us and out the front door. I guess the police did scare him!

WHEN TOO MUCH PRESS IS A BAD THING

There is no other time in a restaurant's history when they will receive more press than when they first open. So, heed this advice. Firstly, get as much press as you can, and market your ass off to keep the momentum going.

The pre-opening press will be great. The pre-opening media should be part of your marketing plans, and the information on the new restaurant should be sent to the same people who will be writing about the restaurant when it opens. The difference will be in the story. Pre-opening will be the excitement of the anticipation of the opening, and the excitement will be creating the buzz for the opening day.

Once the restaurant is open, the buzz should continue. But, remember this: *no buzz, no business.* So, when the opening press and reviews begin to come out, and the gossip escalates, there is a dangerous part of having too much media coverage. If that occurs, the editors, writers, and publishers will wonder why the writers are only writing about the restaurant with the buzz when there are many more openings.

Additionally, there could be a time when it creates challenges for publicists. For instance, if your restaurant is getting all the media attention, it may take writers an extended time to write about other competitors. So, beware because this could be a timing issue for publicists. Good press is excellent, but getting too much too fast may create a predicament for the business.

****

A BUSY BAR CREATES BUZZ!

Does anyone really want to go to a restaurant without any excitement? The answer is no. I have always thought a quiet restaurant is a slow restaurant. *People want to go where people are.* Plus, busy restaurants attract more people. Guests may complain about the noise levels, but when they say, "Wow, this place is packed," it gives good vibes to the restaurant. So, regardless of the restaurant, keep your bar full, and maintain a wait. It will create excellent word-of-mouth marketing for the bar and the restaurant. One more item. The bartenders are key. Change the bartender; lose your regulars. (Poor word-of-mouth)

****

USING THE RESERVATION SYSTEM

When the first reservation systems arrived, I did what I thought was an intelligent thing. I manually added every restaurant reviewer, editor, and writer to the reservation system along with their phone number and a note on the reservation that said, "GET A MANAGER, THIS MAY BE A FOOD WRITER." Then, once the host position printed a dupe for the reservation, the server would have the note in hand, alerting the entire management staff.

****

THOUGHT TO PONDER

Pay your employees better than everyone else. It will show you care about retaining them, and they will like working for you, creating great word-of-mouth amongst your guests.

****

VENDOR MARKETING

✶✶✶✶✶✶✶✶✶✶✶✶✶✶✶✶✶✶✶✶✶✶✶✶✶

12

Vendor marketing is simple. If you are building a new restaurant, during the pre-opening, invite the vendor salespeople in for lunch or dinner. This does a few things. First, they may bring their clients in, and they will help you market the business by introducing new people to the restaurant. And secondly, it helps create buzz for the company. Who do they talk to? Competitors and other people in the industry. Plus, those same people talk to their customers who may be your future guests. So, they can indirectly help pass the word to others that you are open, and the buzz will begin.

So how many types of vendors are there? To name a few: Dry goods, produce, farmers, beer, wine, liquor, paper suppliers, hood companies, cleaning companies, laundry, window cleaners, valet parkers, architect, designer, dish room and kitchen equipment, and the list can go on and on. So, don't let this critical area be forgotten.

13

EMAIL LIST MARKETING

SOFTWARE TO DO THE JOB

Are you looking for email marketing software? My favorite is constantcontact.com, and I have used it for over fifteen years. It's a drag-and-drop site, and you can even schedule the times for the email blast to be sent. There is another email marketing service called Mailchimp.com. These are excellent tools where restaurant owners can help themselves and reduce marketing dollars while increasing profits. Your goal is to create a database of emails.

GUEST EMAILS

One essential item is the gathering of customer emails. While you can have a sign-up page on the website, the second way to get emails from your guests is to hand them a small card to complete & be added to the restaurant email list. One more way is to get them to sign up for your VIP program that offers specials or discounted items.

If you use the card collection item once a day, have the host punch in the emails in your email software and watch the email list grow faster than you have ever seen. Providing the restaurant is busy, this will be the fastest way to *collect* guests' emails. If the restaurant is using a reservation system and the software allows the restaurant to download the emails of the reservations, that is the second-fastest way to collect emails. Download them and then upload them to your email software. Remember this: Email communication with your guest's works. Keep them informed, and you retain them. If you pass on this opportunity, your customers may go elsewhere.

■■■

If email marketing software like Mailchimp or Constant Contact is being used, that's great. Email marketing software reports will show the time and date the receiver opened the email. Why is this important? An opened email tells the business owner who their *active customers* are and who they can market to with additional emails. It also tells them the effectiveness of email marketing. If there is a less than 4% opening rate, the email blasts will need to be reviewed.

Maybe the subject heading needs to be changed? Or perhaps the email is being blacklisted and ending up in the customer's spam? Or perhaps the email lists used are not actual people who have frequented the business. Was the email list purchased? Either way, this data is excellent in knowing the effectiveness of the email marketing efforts.

HOTEL MARKETING

14

RELATIONSHIPS

Having a positive relationship with the local hotels is very important. The reason is simple: They need a place to send their guests, and hotels can keep your restaurant busy on weekday nights. Here are three areas to focus on so they know about the restaurant.

CATERING SALES MANAGERS (CSM)

The catering managers within hotels book large parties. If the hotel is a convention hotel, the parties may amount to hundreds and thousands of guests. Either way, your job is to get to know the CSM in the local hotels. If this means calling them and introducing yourself, then do it. If it means stopping by or even inviting them into the restaurant for a drink and a tour, *then get it going*. Sitting on your hands will not help you.

When you get to know these people, they will remember you as the go-to restaurant that understands how to care for guests. One thing here: Take care of their guests as you would take care of your own. If you have to send out a small appetizer every time, then do it. It will show the

Catering Manager you are taking care of *their guests*. Plus, it makes them look great in their hotel guest's eyes.

One more item. If you have private dining rooms, tell the CSM about it. There are many times the CSM needs off-site dining for their guests.

FRONT DESK, BUILDING/HOTEL CONCIERGES

The front desk managers and staff will also need to know about your restaurant. After all, their guests will be asking for restaurant recommendations, and you want them to send them to your place, right? So how do you get them to send their guests to your business? Similar to the above: Invite the front desk people into your restaurant and buy them lunch or dinner. Hand them menus or appetizer cards. Be sure they have your name as a contact so they can call you.

Additionally, always say yes if and when they call you to get their guests in. The reason is simple. Their guest is probably standing directly in front of them and is listening closely to the conversation. Make the hotel people look like superstars for their guests, and they will reward you many times over.

As for building concierges, there are many of them. First, search for the most significant office buildings in your area. More than likely, there will be a concierge in the building. Then, meet with them and schedule lobby tastings for their tenants.

One more item to mention. Search out and create a database of the Executive Assistants. They book large and small parties for the executives, and developing a relationship with them is highly important.

CHAMBER OF COMMERCE

****

15

The chamber is a great way to meet business people. However, the membership director is the most important person you need to meet. The reason is simple: They get to meet every new member, so their contact list is vast.

Depending on what the chamber of commerce can do for you is a question they have to answer. For example, can they provide your new business with a list of contacts? Can they add your business to a weekly email they send to their members? If they say no, how will they benefit you?

Trying to meet every chamber member would take *years*, so don't even try. It becomes overwhelming. You can host a chamber event at the restaurant and invite the board members. They alone will help you with word-of-mouth marketing and will tell many others. Plus, it will get the members into the restaurant, and you may be able to give them tours and even hand out a goodie bag with menus or a small dessert to go. The critical item here is that the members go to your restaurant and know about its location.

CONVENTION & VISITORS BUREAUS
HOSPITALITY ASSOCIATIONS

****

16

If the restaurant is located in an area with a high volume of convention business, the business should consider joining the convention bureau. The reason is simple. Once the company is a member, they may be privy to the list and contacts of the upcoming convention attendees. This can help with the restaurant marketing to the attendees before ever walking into the state.

If the convention bureau provides the members with the list of upcoming conventions, the list may tell you the number of people, the host hotel, the convention dates, their primary event planner email, and much more. Your job will be to put together a marketing campaign and market to these people. Hopefully, they will include your restaurant in their restaurant lists for their attendees. Lastly, if the convention bureau allows you to place rack cards or brochures in the convention center, you will benefit from the option. Then, when you go to the restaurant's brochures location, you will see your competitors had the same idea.

FINAL THOUGHT

So now you know. It takes a humungous effort to get media coverage. It also takes a tremendous amount of time and planning by publicists, chefs, managers, editors, and publishers. The end game here is to *never stop marketing*. Once you do, people forget about the place of business. So, I'll end it with a few last thoughts.

1. Secure the best location available
2. Create a buzz and keep it buzzing
3. Send press releases with interesting stories out daily
4. Market your ass off
5. Ask yourself daily, "Why did the other restaurant get the press?" After that question, it's time to be more diligent in your marketing.

Best of luck to you in all your endeavors, and I hope you have the busiest restaurant in your area.

****

A note about my company: We develop concepts, train, help, consult, market, and review operations. If there is any need in the restaurant business or a new start-up business, we can help. We also sell our books in bulk to the hospitality industry. Our books led to developing our courses.

Hungry Hospitality also owns Coursini.com (A Restaurant Industry Academy) and helps companies, small or large, in total operations, including start-up, overall sales options, marketing, procedures, and business planning.

Thank you so much for your time. If there is anything my company can do for you or someone you know,

If you are interested in giving us a review on Amazon, we would greatly appreciate the feedback.

To schedule a presentation or training with Cliff Bramble, contact us below. Also, to purchase Cliff's first best-selling book, **The Business Side of Restaurants**, go to Amazon.

Contact

Website

Phone: 678.626.7084 - sales@hungryhospitality.com

****

OKAY, LAST THOUGHT

If, after reading this book, you still need help, we will be happy to help you and get you on the right path to success. It's easy. Call or email us, and we will get back in touch with you within twenty-four hours, and we guarantee you will see a difference in your marketing. Our tiny subscription models keep everyone within their budget. We guarantee it! - sales@hungryhospitality.com

Made in the USA
Middletown, DE
04 December 2023

44686657R00054